# RISKY REEFS IN THE OCEAN OF GLOBAL MARKETS

Common Mistakes of Emerging Markets' Global Expansion

## Stephan S. Sunn

*Davidson Partners*

Copyright © 2024 Stephan Sunn

©Copyright 2024 -2026 Stephan Sun All Rights Reserved

Disclaimer:

This book may not be reproduced or transmitted in any form without the written permission of the authors. Every effort has been made to make this guide as complete and accurate as possible. Although the authors have prepared this guide with the greatest of care, and have made every effort to ensure its accuracy, we assume no responsibility or liability for errors, inaccuracies, or omissions. Before you begin, check with the appropriate authorities to ensure compliance with all laws and regulations. Every effort has been made to make this report as complete and accurate as possible. However, there may be mistakes in typography or content. Also, this report contains information on online marketing and technology only up to the publishing date. Therefore, this report should be used as a guide – not as the ultimate source of Internet marketing information. The purpose of this report is to educate. The authors do not warrant that the information contained in this report is fully complete and shall not be responsible for any errors or omissions. The authors shall have neither liability nor responsibility to any person or entity concerning any loss or damage caused or alleged to be caused directly or indirectly by this report, nor do we make any claims or promises of our ability to generate income by using any of this information.

Davidsons Global Associates & Co. LLC, Davidson, NC 28036, USA    All Inquiries of copyrights, and cooperation go to: Stephan.sunn@aya.yale.edu

# CONTENTS

Title Page
Copyright
Preface
Chapter 1: Emerging Markets' Companies
Chapter 2: Strategic Planning Errors
Chapter 3: Financial Mismanagement
Chapter 4: the Portability of Business Model
Chapter 5: Operational Pitfalls
Chapter 6: Human Resources Challenges
Chapter 7: Errors in Marketing and Sales
Chapter 8: Negligence in Technology and Innovation
Chapter 9 Legal and Ethical Risks
Chapter 10: deficient Risk Assessment and Mitigation
Chapter 11: Short-term Thinking
Chapter 12: Summary and Prospects
Acknowledgement
About The Author
Books By This Author

# Preface

The author and his partners contributing to this series of professional guidance and industry best practices possess over two decades of experience advising multinational corporations and C-suite executives. They are esteemed thought leaders within their respective fields and globally renowned throughout their extensive professional networks. Prior to the COVID-19 pandemic, when international travel was unencumbered, they would convene annually at a rotating global location. Their first reunion following that worldwide crisis was imbued with a profound sense of gratitude for having endured such a cataclysmic event.

Reuniting with one another brought joy to all of us. Even more so, the notion of how delicate and short life began to settle in. The idea of documenting our business experience and lessons, successes or failures, to help our colleagues and clients was formed in 2022 when we gathered in Jamaica. However, with the arrival of ChatGPT and similar trailblazing AI technologies in late 2022, this small proposal gains urgency because we fear within the next decade these revolutionary technologies could transform our lives and society forever, and resemble what COVID-19 has brought to us.

The subject matter of this book series are the business domains we have supported clients worldwide last two decades, with the priority in the last few years. We don't claim we are the researchers or professors in the technologies, but the practitioners who evaluate, choose, and apply state-of-the-art technologies to solve business problems. The technology breakthroughs are not what we pursued, the critical criterion is if the technology solved the business problems with business values. This is why "Case Studies", "Examples" or "Lessons" are weighted much higher than the rigorous analytics of the theories in these business guides.

This book provides a comprehensive roadmap for emerging market companies venturing into global expansion. It highlights common pitfalls across strategic planning, finance, operations, human resources, marketing, technology, legal/ethics, and risk management. The book emphasizes thorough market research, cultural adaptation, local partnerships, brand building, innovation investment, and long-term vision.

As the global landscape evolves, it anticipates trends like digitization, sustainability integration, and talent acquisition challenges. The book provides corporate decision-makers with insights and best practices to navigate complexities, mitigate risks, and foster sustainable growth while driving innovation and progress internationally.

# Chapter 1: Emerging Markets' Companies

With the rapid pace of change in today's business world, the global expansion of companies from emerging markets has become a critical strategic imperative for achieving sustainable growth and maintaining competitive advantage.

As they solidify their leadership positions in their home markets, emerging market companies are recognizing that they have to look beyond their borders to the world at large. The chance to reach new customers, tap the global pool of talent and resources, and diversify revenue streams impels them to set forth on the difficult but potentially immensely rewarding journey of going global.

Companies often decide to launch international operations after they have succeeded within their home market. These companies have shown that they can innovate, be adaptable, and thrive while operating under domestic constraints. They have built up the confidence, and the ambition, to take their proven success formulas global. However, globalizing a company requires far more than importing a domestic formula. Indeed, the mindset and the strategic skills demanded by different international environments are so distinct, as one BCG leader told us, that acquiring them can feel like "repatriating after long exile on another planet."

Emerging market companies looking to successfully advance into the global marketplace need to first reframe their vision and mission in order to account for a wider-reaching, international focus. This involves performing thorough market research to distinguish major customer segments, to recognize these segments' particular wants and needs, and fashion unique selling propositions that communicate across various cultural and economic systems. By marrying their core competencies with the exigencies of global demand trends, these companies can successfully position themselves for their target regions in foreign markets.

Advantages of Emerging Markets Although plenty of issues crop up for businesses that try to expand into new countries, there are also loads of poor countries realizing the rewards of global business. Take the following insight: firms from emerging markets frequently have a competitive edge that equips them to impress globally. One of the most conspicuous advantages these companies have is agility and adaptability. Where firms from advanced economies frequently have difficulty adjusting, companies from weaker economies have been conducting business amid instability and anarchy for years. For these businesses, change — and the opportunity it brings — is just part of business as usual.

Not only are emerging-market firms often more agile, but they can also be cost competitive. Lower labor and production costs in their home countries —the result of cheaper wages and less-regulated markets—give them an edge that's particularly powerful when they enter price-sensitive markets or take on incumbents with heavy fixed and high overhead costs. By exploiting this advantage, they can underprice incumbents and reset market dynamics.

Furthermore, many companies in developing countries have mastered the art of devising innovative solutions that can address the unique problems that their local customers encounter. The outcome, usually a result of a thorough understanding of the environment and local shortages, could then be employed to deal with similar issues in other markets with emerging qualities. Once that has been done and the businesses can cater to the untapped or ignored market segments, they can differentiate themselves and discover a brand new market.

Challenges and Opportunities As emerging market companies look to move out of their domestic comfort zone and onto the worldwide stage, they'll have to deal with a whole new range of challenges and opportunities. One of the biggest challenges is understanding and adjusting to the special regulatory, cultural, and competitive dynamics of developed markets. Those markets tend to have stricter regulation, more demanding customers, and a host of strong, smart competitors that know the rules of the game inside and out.

In order to surmount these difficulties, firms from emerging markets must devote resources to exhaustive market research, establish robust partnerships with local firms, and demonstrate a sophisticated grasp of the legal and cultural environment. This can mean hiring local employees, forging tactical alliances with relevant stakeholders, and reshaping products, services, and marketing efforts to reflect the preferences of the target market.

Amongst the challenges, we can identify some significant opportunities. Emerging market firms have the ability to identify underserved market segments and leverage their unique strengths to differentiate themselves. For example, a firm with a deep understanding of the needs and preferences of consumers in its home market may be able to develop products or services that cater to underserved ethnic or immigrant communities in developed markets. By focusing on niches and leveraging their cultural insights, these firms can carve out profitable positions even in the most competitive markets.

In subsequent chapters, we shall study emerging market corporations' typical blunders in their global expansion endeavors as well as discuss pragmatic approaches to surmounting these obstacles. Either from strategical plotting and financial administration or operational contemplation and marketing ploys, this guide aims to furnish emerging market managers with the knowledge and experience to maneuver through the intricate realm of global business expansion and successes in worldwide markets for the long haul.

# Chapter 2: Strategic Planning Errors

When emerging market companies begin their global expansion, one of the most crucial elements is the quality of their strategic planning, and it can effectively decide their success or failure in the operation. A qualified and comprehensive strategic plan functions as a map, leading the company to get across the complicated global market, and harnessing resources effectively to achieve the expected results. Nevertheless, a lot of emerging market firms neglected the process of strategy planning and made unnecessary mistakes as they stretched out, which may impede and destroy their way of doing things. So, many emerging market companies have questions about "What to do next."

One of the main strategic planning errors that emerging markets companies usually commit is not conducting adequate market research and analysis. Many companies jump directly into international expansion without carefully examining their target markets. As a result, they lack a profound understanding of the local business environment, consumer behavior, and other forces in the competitive market.

Not having this market intelligence can produce a few harmful outcomes. Initially, companies may undervalue the divergence in cultural and financial factors between their home market and the one they are trying to sell a good or service in. This leads to misaligned product offerings, pricing strategies, and marketing messages. Second, they may overrate the reputation of their products or services in the market they are entering. This happens in the form of unrealistic sales projections and how they allocate their resources. Lastly, if companies do not know the competition in the market or see that they are doing the same thing, then they will not stand out to the customer and won't be able to get a hold of any part of that market.

In order to avoid these traps, emerging-market companies must make a commitment to thorough market research and analysis as a fundamental element of their strategic planning process. This means investing in both primary and secondary research, such as consumer surveys, focus groups, and in-depth interviews with industry experts and prospective customers. This data collection and analysis will yield a better understanding of the market opportunity, barriers to entry and channel strategy, and the identification of the unique characteristics of each target market that will necessitate different strategies.

Additionally, another common mistake when it comes to strategic planning is that way organizations create their global strategy incorrectly and not flexibly. Particularly with emerging market companies, as they grow, they expand internationally in an incremental way. In other words, they react opportunistically. The result of this is a fragmented approach to creating a global footprint. What tend to see is that these companies go into too many markets, they pick up lots of balls at once before they develop any real capabilities. And what's even worse is that they later find out most of the balls have been dropped and they usually run out of money. So, that's where you see the lack of clarity, and the lack of sequencing causing real disturbance.

Emerging market companies that seek to prosper in the worldwide market must first craft a full global strategy that is consistent with their centering administrative plans and capabilities. This strategy begins with a comprehensive assessment of the strengths, weaknesses, opportunities, and threats (SWOT) that the company faces in the global market. It enables the company to pivot quickly in response to changing circumstances or new openings.

A global strategy that is easy to understand should spell out exactly what it is that needs to be accomplished both globally and for each target market as well, and it should provide a clear roadmap of how to accomplish it, including how to allocate resources and how to enter new markets and continue to operate in existing markets. Additionally, it should think about the future and build into the plan the ways that the company's international presence can be sustainable, scalable and strong enough to support the growth that the company anticipates.

Another common strategic planning error committed by emerging market companies is miscalculating the competitive landscape in foreign markets.

Most of these companies believe that their market dominance in the home country gives them a competitive edge in the global markets. Therefore, they typically overlook local firms' capabilities and strengths, assuming that overmatched.

This mistake can be costly. In general, local rivals often comprehend how the market works, have a close connection with crucial stakeholders and hold a well-established brand name. Additionally, local companies can be better while coping with strong legal and regulatory surroundings and cultural and language hurdles. Even if businesses have dealt with far-away operations, it is difficult to fully control every aspect of complicated distant operations.

To avoid underestimating the competition, an emerging market firm must do a comprehensive competitive analysis during the strategic planning stage. This includes locating the key competitors in each market segment, comparing their strengths and weaknesses with those of the firm, and formulating strategies to separate our product/service offerings and value proposition from our rivals. This may also entail establishing strategic alliances or partnerships with local players to gain knowledge about the market, points of access to the distribution system, and other important assets.

Emerging market firms can build a platform for successful expansion by investing in thorough market research, by developing a clear and flexible global strategy and by conducting accurate competition assessments. In the chapters ahead, we will investigate other strategic issues, including money management, operation planning and marketing tools, that can help emerging market firms tap the complexities and possibilities of the global enterprise.

# Chapter 3: Financial Mismanagement

One of the most significant challenges faced by emerging market companies as they step into the global marketplace is to critically appraise their financial resources. A global expansion calls for a sizeable investment of financial capital. Such financial outlets provide well-established companies employed but even they can find themselves stretched as they manage the complexities of international finance. Misguided management of finances can rapidly turn a company's global ambitions into a failure, resulting in foregone opportunities, impaired credibility, and possible financial collapse.

One of the common financial mistakes that are made by emerging market companies today is to underestimate the true financial cost of global expansion. Many companies don't look at the full range of expenses that exist when entering new markets like market scenario, legal and regulatory environment, local staff and admin, setting up infrastructure, etc.

Various negative impacts can be caused by the lack of financial planning. First, companies may have insufficient retained earnings in order to finance their international operations, therefore, having cash flow problems and no flexibility in their finance. Second, if there is poor budgeting and forecasting, companies may have unrealistic expectations and have a wrong resource allocation making companies difficult to execute their global strategy.

In order to sidestep these risks, emerging market firms must build extensive financial plans that accurately reflect the expenses of worldwide development. This involves extensive research of the financial requirements of each target market including the cost of entry into the market, the cost of ongoing operations and the cost of potential contingencies. It also involves the implementation of rigorous budgeting and forecasting processes so that the company is able to monitor their financial performance and make reasoned decisions on how resources are to be allocated.

Another pervasively common financial mistake that emerging market enterprises make is the tendency to neglect currency risks and fluctuations in foreign exchange rates. Companies, in their pursuit of entering new and greener pastures, often come across a number of currency issues, comprising transaction risks, translation risks, and economic risks.

There are transaction risks when a firm engages in business dealings using a foreign currency. This exposes the corporation to potential losses in light of unfavorable exchange rate movement. Without an effective evaluation of a company's translation risk, a corporation could have difficulties in tracking its financial performance. What is more, economic risks have a broad impact from changes in exchange rates on corporate competitiveness and profitability in operating activities abroad.

To reduce these risks, companies in emerging markets must have strong currency risk management strategies. This may mean executing hedging strategies, where a forward contract or currency options, are used to safeguard against unfavorable exchange rate moves. It may also call for setting pricing strategies and profit margins to allow for currency changes and preserve the ability to compete in foreign markets.

Tax planning and compliance issues are common because cross-border expansion subjects a company to complex and potentially contradictory tax regulations. The taxes that cause the biggest headaches include value-added taxes (VAT), corporate income taxes, and withholding taxes. Many countries impose VAT on transactions at rates as high as 25%. Countries in emerging markets typically have higher, more complex tax regimes, including substantial and complex VATs. Emerging-market governments often use these taxes as public-hidden taxes that raise revenue from the freewheeling retail sector, which sometimes operates as a virtual underground economy. Progressive and ambitious finance ministers in some emerging-market countries are now trying to capture more value in their VAT gold mines, including enforcing a VAT incompatible with the offending financial compliers' accounting systems. Large international companies know the tax man taketh but also giveth and must first know how to properly avoid or limit the taketh to then arrange a give some-back maneuver so as to sustain the commercial reward or success system. We lawyers at my firm see audits of foreign businesses with past due VAT reporting or absence of total VAT amounts paid or in hand ranging into the $millions for a mere project some of our Chinese retainers have started. None of these for now fun and games audits with extraterritorial drawback of VAT money and jammed up VAT tech; surely no one in their right financial mind would even think such a tax gambit possible!? Emerging-market VATs, as a group, are almost childishly simple compared to U.S. sales-and-use taxes, never mind the average of several western VAT regimes reporting a return nearly as user-friendly as an IRS Form 1040 shalt not be accomplished. Emerging markets companies expanding globally now can have far less withholding, VAT and income tax with investigation board-level tax with confidence and Chief Financial Officer driven worldwide tax planning in place. We work with you on tax implementation anywhere in the world to provide you with the Jack Palance "Dracula" tax savings.

Unless these laws are well understood and taken on board, penalties, legislation and stigma loom large. It can also mean missing out on opportunities to optimize your tax load, such as the use of double taxation treaties or structuring your global operations for maximum tax efficiency.

To steer clear of these tripwires, it is imperative for developing market businesses to put tax planning and compliance at the top of the agenda on their financial management strategy, including working with local tax professionals and advisors to learn the tax regulations in each target market, setting up strong internal tax reporting and compliance mechanisms, and in some cases, restructuring its global operations or setting up foreign subsidiaries to optimize its global tax profile.

In order to secure a strong financial foundation for their global expansion endeavors, companies originating in emerging markets must construct comprehensive financial plans for the future. We will discuss similar financial issues of concern to global managers in this chapter and the following chapter. Core issues such as capital allocation and financial performance monitoring continue to plague international managers because of their innate opaqueness. In addition to these issues, emerging market managers should also carefully review their tax planning and compliance activities, develop effective currency risk management programs, educate senior executives and outside shareholders on the principles of value-based management, and develop detailed financial plans. This global recipe, if followed, gives emerging market companies the best opportunity for establishing a solid, stable financial platform for their global expansion activities.

# CHAPTER 4: THE PORTABILITY OF BUSINESS MODEL

When expanding globally, emerging market companies often fail to realize that their domestic business models will work well in foreign markets. The companies wrongly think that what has helped them succeed in one specific country will do the same in any new country, leading to thinking that hinders their adaptation and ability to succeed in new markets.

One of the most common mistakes emerging market companies make is assuming that a business model that has been successful in their home market will automatically work in foreign markets. This assumption often comes from a lack of appreciation for the fact that each market is unique in both its cultural, economic, and regulatory factors.

For instance, a firm that has thrived on a low-priced, high-quantity company model at home may have trouble emulating this tactic abroad. A bank that has used informal networks and personal connections to sell loans to domestic customers may struggle to build a similar network overseas, particularly in a country where business practices and decision processes are highly formal and impersonal.

In order to avoid this error, businesses in emerging markets need to think anew in each new market that they go into; they must do their research and find out what it takes to be successful in the market. That could mean modifying their model to closely match the local business environment, including adjusting price points, offering different products, or re-tooling the supply chain.

Neglecting to Adjust Pricing Strategies for Local Economic Conditions and Competitive Scenarios It is a common blunder amongst emerging market corporations that they fail to adapt their pricing strategies in response to local economic conditions and competitive scenarios. Companies often mistakenly assume that the pricing strategies which worked in their homeland will be successful in foreign countries, without considering the factors that influence pricing in each market.

For instance, a firm that has achieved its triumph with a premium pricing strategy in its domestic market may counter problems in maintaining this method in a foreign market where the average income is lower and consumers are more price-sensitive. Also, a firm that is dependent on a penetration pricing strategy to distinguish its penetration pricing strategy from the same-market competitors may face problems in supporting this method in a foreign market where the competition may be more established and barriers to entry are higher.

One way to avoid this mistake is for emerging-market companies to craft pricing strategies based on the specific economic conditions and competitive dynamics of each targeted market. This could entail conducting market research to gauge local preferences and the local's capacity for spending, as well as analyzing the pricing strategies of key rivals. It also might require adjusting profit margins or exploring new revenue models to ensure competitiveness and profitability in every market.

Another error frequently committed by emerging market firms engaging in defense industry transfer initiatives is the undervaluing of the logistical, supply chain management, and distribution costs and complications indigenous to new markets. Many firms assume that their domestic supply chain and distribution networks can be seamlessly transferred abroad, and fail to consider the idiosyncratic infrastructure, regulatory, and cultural factors that can affect these processes.

To illustrate, a corporation that has fostered its triumph on a centered allotment model within its base market could find it arduous to keep this approach in an outland market with a scarcer enhanced transportation infrastructure or further multifaceted customs decrees. Correspondingly, a corporation that has leaned upon an unaccompanied supplier or manufacturer within its base market might expose itself to difficulty with executing creditable furnish series liaisons within an outland market with distinct business practices and quality benchmarks.

In order to prevent this misstep, companies emerging in international markets must conduct thorough research to understand the logistics, supply chain, and distribution challenges and opportunities of each targeted market. The companies might partner with local partners or experts in order to manage the guidelines and principles of the territory, form steady supply-chain networks, and use adequate delivery tactics. It might also require the companies to invest in new technologies or assets to secure maximum supply chain efficacy and maximized delivery to each market.

Another issue is when growing market firms don't develop a localized marketing and branding strategy for each target market. Many firms assume that the domestic marketing and branding technique will be enough and they don't factor in the unique languages, cultures, and consumer preferences that shape the brand.

Let's take the case examples. A company that has based its brand on a cultural or linguistic identity that resonates with consumers in its home market may struggle to take that positioning into a foreign market. There, consumers may have different cultural values or language preferences that make the strategy less effective. For example, Gap Inc., the American clothing store, initially stumbled when it tried to export its red, white and blue clothing and imagery to Europe. The aesthetic is about as overtly American as it gets. Gap eventually had to shift strategies and recognize that European consumers don't value American styling the way Americans do—they found the approach obnoxious, and they wanted something more refined. Similarly, what works in one marketing channel or with one message in a home market may not be exportable to other markets. A company that has articulated its messaging around one channel and marketing "story" will hit barriers when it tries to engage consumers in a foreign market, where media consumption habits and advertising norms differ. GateHouse Media, the American newspaper company that sought to make money by sucking as much as it could out of local newspaper properties, couldn't make its strategy work when it expanded to local papers within the U.K. Those operations are run somewhat like little more than cottage industries, and U.S. audiences are more advertiser-friendly. Neither of those approaches works well in the U.K., and the pulpit from which

GateHouse spoke in the U.S.—advertising revenue—just didn't exist in the U.K.

In order to prevent this error from occurring, it is necessary for emerging-market companies to generate marketing and branding plans that are specifically based on the cultural, linguistic, and consumer preferences of a targeted market. This involves conducting market research to understand consumer attitudes and behaviors within a certain country, as well as collaborating with local advertising and marketing partners to create a message that holds a valuable connection to the targeted market's culture.

To improve their chances of succeeding in the global market, companies in emerging markets need to recognize the shortcomings of their domestic business model and be able to adjust their strategies to properly deal with the unique challenges and opportunities of each specific target market. In the following chapters, we will discuss other important considerations to take into account for a successful expansion worldwide, especially the developed countries, such as talent management, risk mitigation, and long-term sustainability.

# Chapter 5: Operational Pitfalls

When emerging market firms partner to enter foreign markets they often find themselves struggling to overcome a range of operational snags that threaten their chances of success. From navigating complex supply chain and logistics networks to maintaining regulatory compliance, from configuring products and services to meet local requirements to managing local human resources regulations and practices, the operational terrain of global expansion is fraught with pitfalls. In this chapter, we will review some of the more typical operational mistakes made by emerging market firms, and consider some prescriptions for overcoming these challenges.

Supply chain and logistics planning deficiencies are a problem for many companies operating in emerging markets. Managers of these companies often do not realize how difficult and expensive sourcing, manufacturing, and distributing products across borders can be; as a result, inefficiencies increase, risks and delays persist, and these deficiencies become a major headache

Emergent market firms frequently commit the error of misunderstanding the costs and times associated with shipping. Executives might believe that they can just graft their domestic logistics and shipping systems onto foreign markets without thinking about the idiosyncratic infrastructure, geographic, regulatory, and transportation considerations that can affect when and how goods are delivered and distributed. As a result, supplies may run out, customer shipments can be delayed, and the expense of getting goods through customs and to end customers will balloon. In all of these cases, profits have been eroded and customers have been reviled.

Another challenge is the absence of local assembly and dissemination networks. In a lot of developing marketplaces, companies do not have a local presence to be founded, which is nearly impossible to achieve or expense effectively in overseas markets. As a result, these companies may lack the substructure necessary to promptly respond to marketplace transformations. Consequently, they may have knowledge of stockouts or overcapacity. They may also be burdened with increased conveyance and supply times, which could hurt customer satisfaction and dependence.

In order to avoid these dangers, companies in emerging markets must spend money on strong supply chain and logistics planning. They will have to look at each target market separately. They may need to work with the local logistics partners or even set up their own warehouses and distribution networks in that area to keep response times at the best and transportation costs very low. They could even have to invest in supply chain visibility to track potential dangers and manage those dangers to keep them at a minimum

Neglecting Local Regulatory and Compliance Matters It is also a regular failure of emerging market companies to take into account local regulatory and compliance matters. Many companies assume that their home market compliance processes and standards will be adequate in foreign markets. They do not know the unique legal, regulatory, and cultural factors that influence their operations.

A common mistake is the non-compliance with regulations on import and export. This is because every country does have its own customs procedures, documentation requirements and tariffs which differ according to the product category, the country of origin, and the purpose for which they are being imported or used. The outcome of this could be customs detentions, fines, and delays, all of which can obliterate supply chains and the reputation of the company.

Product recalls legal repercussions, and reputation harm are just some of the consequences of an inability to obtain required certifications or fulfill home-country standards.

To surmount such challenges, firms attempting to globalize from their emerging market homes must make regulatory and compliance planning central to their strategy. They should consider working with in-country legal and compliance experts to comprehend every specific market's regulatory matrix. They should have sturdy management systems and procedures in place to ensure consistent, local compliance. They should work to establish clear communication and accountability lines between home and foreign staff so that reporting and documentation can be handled quickly but also to the most precise standards.

Weak Localization A third operational pitfall that emerging market companies are prone to is the inability to adapt their products and services to local market needs and preferences. Many companies presume that their domestic product offerings will be as attractive to foreign consumers as they are to domestic ones, without examining the unique cultural, linguistic, and environmental factors that influence local market demand.

One error involves ignoring local tastes and preferences. Consumer preferences can differ significantly across various markets, affected by aspects such as cultural values, social norms, and economic conditions. Failing to adapt products and services to local market preferences can restrict their appeal and competitiveness, resulting in reduced sales and market share.

Additionally, another error is insufficient personalization and localization. A lot of companies in rapidly evolving markets don't fully appreciate the importance of tailoring their products, packaging, and advertising to make them more appealing to local patrons. That means translating ingredients and instructions, redesigning (and sometimes shrinking) packages, and even getting product formulas to conform with local ingredient or labeling requirements.

In order to prevent these issues from arising, firms from developing countries need to pay attention to adapting goods and services as a main part of their approach to growth in global markets. This will entail being systematically aware of how consumers in other countries like to behave and what they want by doing extensive market research. They would also need to work with local employees or partners to create and test product and service offerings that fit with what potential customers in other countries are looking for. Finally, it would require investment in flexible manufacturing and supply chain systems which allow quick and inexpensive adaptation to customer needs.

Emerging market firms can improve their likelihood of success in the global marketplace by addressing these operational challenges proactively and making the necessary process, partnership, and capability investments. In the following chapters, we will further explore operational considerations that rise above the novel operational problems of emerging markets, including talent management, technology adoption, and continuous improvement strategies to optimize global operations and promote firm growth in emerging markets.

# Chapter 6: Human Resources Challenges

When emerging-market organizations invest in overseas expansion, they frequently encounter considerable human resources (HR) difficulties that impair their ability to draw, manage, and nurture the staff essential for achievement in a global business climate. From comprehending cultural variances to constructing efficient cross-border crews, the HR realm of global expansion is bewildering and steadily changing. In this unit, we will inspect numerous of the most commonly committed HR mistakes by emerging-market organizations and inspect how to save ourselves from these obstacles.

Improper Hiring and Talent Management Plans

One mistake that is costing emerging-market companies valuable human capital is failing to understand the nuances of the labor market, including the available pool of skilled talent, delayed organizational structures driven by competition, and cultural expectations related to job scope and responsibilities. This oversight frequently results in mismatched hiring criteria, uncompetitive job offers, and high turnover, all of which can neutralize the growth of a strong, locally-based workforce. A separate pitfall is undervaluing the bearing of cultural congruity in contracting and talent management. Each market has its unusual cultural mores and standards that shape employee behaviors, attitudes, and hopes. If we don't recognize these cultural factors in contracting and talent management, we're increasing the risk of having uneven expectations, muddled communication, lessening commitment for an employee, and bringing down productivity.

To avoid these challenges, brands expanding onto emerging markets need to invest in developing a thorough understanding of local labor market dynamics and local cultural factors in each of their target markets. They may need to engage with local HR partners or consultants to create customized recruitment and talent management strategies that align with local market requirements and expectations. They could adjust job descriptions, compensation packages, and performance management procedures to match local cultural norms and social values closer.

Another HR mistake that emerging market companies frequently make is that they do not invest enough in training and development programs for their global workforce. A lot of companies believe that the training programs in the domestic markets will be as effective in foreign markets, without considering the of their employees in the foreign market.

Paying no attention to the need for local expertise and knowledge is a downfall. Every market has its unique set of business practices, regulatory requirements, and customer expectations, which employees have to understand and navigate effectively. The inability to deliver specific training and development programs that help build local expertise keeps employees restricted in their ability to execute accordingly and adjust to local market conditions.

Another drawback is found in the lack of a developing commitment and retaining the employees. Many firms in emerging markets rather focus their human resource initiatives towards hiring and boarding, where they neglect the long-term development and commitment towards their workforce across the globe. This may lead to personnel attrition, declining commitment, and no further growth development pipeline for the firm's soon-to-be worldwide expansion.

To avoid such issues, it becomes imperative for emerging market firms to embed training and development as part of their global HR strategy. This can be achieved by designing specialized training programs to develop specific local knowledge and skills. Another way can be to support continuous learning and development by providing growth and retention opportunities. Also, it can be through collaboration with local educational institutions or training providers to develop custom programs tailored to meet the distinct needs of the local workforce.

Another challenge that often emerges for HR in emerging market companies is developing effective leadership and management practices in a global business environment. Many companies use an expatriate approach to staffing. An expatriate is a citizen of one country employed in another country by an organization headquartered in the first country. Expatriate managers are assigned to perform a third-country service in a foreign country.

Companies often fill key management positions in a foreign unit with managers from their head office in an appropriate place at an assigned time. Many companies select an expatriate manager for a foreign operation. leading their foreign operations, without understanding the cultural and communication difficulties of managing across borders. An expatriate manager is a citizen of one country employed in another country by an organization headquartered in the first country. Often, a reward package is offered to the family members of expatriates. Expatriate managers are assigned to perform a third-country service in a foreign country.

Relying too heavily upon expatriate management is one error. While expatriate managers can bring a lot of expertise and experience to a foreign operation, they might not succeed in adapting to local cultural norms and expectations. Therefore, team effectiveness can falter and communication can break down. In addition, it might be challenging for them to establish trust and credibility among local employees and stakeholders.

Failing to empower local leaders and decision-makers is another. Many multinational companies in emerging markets micro-manage their overseas operations, centralizing authority and limiting the power and ability of local managers and teams to decide. As a result, local businesses lack the agility, innovation, and empathy with local market needs and eventually breed higher attrition rates among local employees.

In order to prevent these errors, up-and-coming companies in emerging markets should focus on developing regional leadership and worldwide control abilities that provide a middle ground between adapting to and remaining true to the local condition. For example, they might need to pay attention to cross-cultural training and executive development programs for both expat and local staff – as well as clear decision-making rights,-roles, and responsibilities that enable local teams to drive business performance. Furthermore, they should focus on having a strong pipeline of leaders, making sure enough people are rising in the ranks to fill needed roles.

By addressing these HR challenges proactively and by investing in the necessary strategies, programs and capabilities, emerging market companies can build and retain a strong global workforce that propels long-term business success. In the forthcoming chapters, we will examine additional HR issues including diversity and inclusion, employee engagement, and HR technology and analytics. These topics will help emerging market companies optimize their global HR practices and support their international growth goals.

# CHAPTER 7: ERRORS IN MARKETING AND SALES

When emerging-market firms go overseas, they often find themselves struggling with the grueling challenges of marketing and selling. This can stymie their ability to build brand, create demand, and drive revenue growth. From crafting effective marketing strategies, to building customer relationships, the marketing and sales landscape for global expansion is complex and ever-evolving. In this chapter, we take a closer look at some of the most common marketing and sales blunders that emerging-market companies make as they enter foreign markets, and present some ways in which emerging-market companies avoid them.

One of the most daunting challenges for emerging-market companies is the new imperative to develop and execute marketing strategies that resonate with local customers and make money for the company. Far too often, companies underestimate the complexity and significance of local market dynamics, leading them to deploy misaligned marketing messages, channels, and tactics.

An error that is often made by businesses in emerging markets is that they do not have enough knowledge about customers' behaviors and preferences in the local market. Each market in which businesses are operating is separated, and different by culture, society, and economy, and it also shapes customers' attitudes, behaviors, and decision-making processes itself. If companies do not pay attention to market research and customer segmentation, then they will apply the worn-out or common marketing approach which has no meaning and purpose in the local market.

Another mistake comes in the form of marketing channels and tactics not being used effectively. Most of the new market companies make use of the same marketing channels and tactics as in their domestic markets without taking into account the entertainment styles and choices of the local customers. As a result, client engagement is low, marketing dollars are wasted, and target markets are missed and under-influenced

For emerging market companies to steer clear of these slipups, they must commit to acquiring a profound comprehension of the discrete customer culture and appetites of the customers within each market they seek to occupy. This can necessitate running original market research, such as surveys, focus groups, and ethnographic studies with customers, as well as analyzing secondary market data and competitive intelligence. Etihad Airways, for instance, discovered via surveys of its own customers in Australia that Americans' favorite "guilty pleasure" movies were the very ones that Australians enjoyed least of all. Likewise, performing novel market research may mandate developing focused customer segments--and personas— as drivers behind marketing strategy and tactics. For example, one national fast-food chain in Brazil concluded that the two "millennial" groups, which together consume nearly half of all fast food in Brazil—"its" (persons), as they are called, and the newly emerging "curbers"—had distinct attitudes towards fast-food dining, so their menu's ambiance and branding needed to be distinct too.

Ineffectual Market Introduction Strategies are how an up-and-coming firm commits another major marketing and sales mistake. This happens when an organization makes inadequate plans for its market introduction into foreign countries. The majority of organizations fail to appreciate the intricacies and significance of launch planning and consequently produce results that fall short and forfeit the growth opportunity that the initial launch provides.

Choosing the wrong entry mode could prove to be a costly mistake. Joint ventures, acquisitions, and greenfield investments all need to be evaluated separately. Each has its own advantages and disadvantages, costs and risks. For a company to get it right, it must assess the plusses and minuses of each in light of its particular business objectives, internal resources, and host-country circumstances. Guess wrong and a company faces punishing outlays, operational problems, and weak market backing.

In addition, another possible error is the exclusion of critical strategic alliances and arrangements that may expedite market entry as well as ensure rapid growth. A number of emerging market enterprises venture abroad through solo efforts, forfeiting local wisdom, contacts, as well as capabilities that could be derived from potential collaborations with strategic partners. As a result, the time to market elongates, the so-called 'cost of entry' rises and one's ability to compete with local players usually slackens.

In order to avoid these traps, the managerial task is to develop a comprehensive market entry plan that evaluates various possible entry modes, identifies potential partners and alliances, and coordinates the entry mode with the company's overall business strategy or objectives. This may involve conducting thorough due diligence on potential partners, developing clear legal agreements and governance structures, and investing in ongoing relationship management and communication.

One further obstacle to marketing and selling abroad is delivering adequate customer service and support in target foreign markets. Many emerging market companies underestimate the importance of local language support, cultural adaptation, and responsive customer service in building and maintaining strong customer relationships that drive long-term growth.

An oversight is when you disregard the significance of local language support in customer engagements. In emerging markets, many companies use English or native languages to communicate with their customers. However, not paying attention to the language preferences and habits of the customers may create a barrier, therefore reducing the conversation level, and finally decreasing customer satisfaction, and as a result, leading to the withdrawal of customers.

Another conspicuous absence is the lack of strong after-sale customer service and support systems in overseas markets. A lot of companies from emerging markets concentrate their energies on acquiring new customers and ignore the infrastructure and processes needed to maintain and amplify existing customer relationships. The result is often high churn, negative word of mouth and abridged customer lives.

In order to avoid these risks, companies in emerging markets need to give customer service a high priority and make it a core component of their marketing and sales strategy. This may mean investing in local language support capabilities, such as hiring native-speaking customer support reps or aligning with local language service providers. Additionally, investing could include building local after-sales service networks, such as warranty support, repair services and customer training programs, to ensure that customer concerns are resolved quickly and with accurate results.

Although companies that are just entering the international market will face barriers in sales and marketing, they can surmount them by addressing proactively the four dimensions of marketing and sales and by making the required strategic and capability investments and partnerships. In so doing, they build strong customer relationships, revenue streams, and brands. In subsequent chapters, we will explore other marketing and sales challenges —sales enablement, digital marketing, and customer experience management—that will help developing market companies move into the next era of their global marketing and sales efforts, creating long-term equity value and optimizing long-term growth.

# CHAPTER 8: NEGLIGENCE IN TECHNOLOGY AND INNOVATION

In today's fast-changing global business environment, technology and innovation are key drivers of competitive advantage and growth For companies to expand into foreign markets, technology infrastructure and innovation processes often fail to adapt to the specific requirements and expectations of local customers and stakeholders. Our goal in this chapter is to analyze the most prevalent technology and innovation pitfalls that companies face while expanding into foreign markets and to offer a set of strategies for managing and mitigating these challenges.

Absence of a technological adaptation infrastructure, the most difficult technology challenge emerging-market companies face is reengineering their technology infrastructure to accommodate the idiosyncratic features of foreign markets. Many companies believe that the technology stack and processes that served them well in their home markets will translate effortlessly to the foreign ones, without considering the differing technologies, regulations, and user preferences at either end.

Overlooking local technological advancements and infrastructure is an error. Many emerging markets have skipped traditional technology adoption curves and created their own technology ecosystems and standards. Not adapting to these advancements can cause compatibility problems, reduced performance, and lower user adoption rates.

One more possible weak point is the consequence of failing to exploit local innovation ecosystems and talent pools. Many of the emerging markets have highly developed startup and innovation communities where they can learn insights, associations, and flow of relevant people for foreign companies. Disregarding the actions to encourage these local innovation ecosystems can miss many collaboration, co-creation, and market-relevant innovation activities.

To prevent these hazards, Firms in emerging markets must make investments now in building a deep and surrounding knowledge of the local technology landscape and user preferences in each target market. That may mean subjecting technology to rigorous tests, partnering with and paying local technology partners and experts, and adapting technology infrastructure and processes to meet individual local requirements and standards. It may also mean assembling local innovation capabilities such as research and development centers, innovation labs, or startup accelerators to draw on local talent and knowledge.

Insufficient cybersecurity measures are an additional technology oversight committed by emerging market companies that do not establish adequate cybersecurity measures in foreign markets. Emerging market firms often underestimate the cybersecurity risks and threats in these markets, which can leave vulnerabilities open for potential data breaches. Being hacked in these markets can damage a company's reputation and mission-critical financial performance.

Another pitfall is not fully grasping regional cyber threats and attack vectors. Various rising markets present dissimilar cybersecurity challenges, from weak regulatory structures to under-resourced enforcement and entrenched cybercriminal and espionage networks. Dismissing or failing to mitigate these local cyber threats puts businesses in danger of targeted attacks, data exfiltration, or other cyber incidents.

Just as dangerous is the problem of inadequate privacy and data protection compliance. A lot of markets during expansion have differing privacy and data protection rules and regulations than those that exist in more advanced markets like the EU's General Data Protection Regulation. By disregarding these particular data protection requirements and privacy requirements of these countries, one might run into some lawful, financial penalties.

To steer clear of these dangers, emerging market enterprises must recognize cybersecurity and data protection as a crucial element of their worldwide IT strategy. This could embrace performing a methodical cybersecurity risk assessment, introducing strong cybersecurity controls and incident response arrangements, and starting cybersecurity discipline for workers. It might oblige also to put money into local data protection and privacy skills, like selecting domestic data protection officers or collaborating with domestic legal and compliance businesses.

Third, emerging-market companies often struggle to develop and execute effective strategies for digital transformation in host-country markets. Companies frequently underestimate the complexity and criticality of local digital ecosystems and user behavior, leading to misaligned digital initiatives and investments.

An error would be not being in line with the local digital trends and user preferences. Many emerging markets have unique digital adoption patterns and user behavior that are unlike the developed markets. Failure to comprehend and be in line with the local digital trends and preferences can lead to low user engagement, a poor customer experience and a reduced digital ROI.

Another error is not being integrated with local digital platforms and ecosystems. In plenty of developing markets, there are different digital platforms and ecosystems like social networks, online marketplaces, and mobile payment systems, all of which can be inherited completely from other countries. Neglecting these countless local digital platforms and ecosystems implies that companies cannot contact and connect to local users and partners. So, it seems to reduce a lot of chances for companies to acquire new customers and partners in these markets.

To sidestep these errors, emerging market firms must outline a robust digital transformation strategy harmonious with native market needs and desires. This might entail running extensive market research and user tests in order to fathom local digital behaviors and choices. It could also involve launching distinctive digital projects and promotions targeted to local users. In addition, it might ask for cultivating local digital competencies and cooperation, including employing local digital mastery, working with local digital agencies, or purchasing local digital start-ups.

By taking the initiative to tackle these technology and innovation challenges and investing in the right strategies, capabilities and partnerships, emerging-market companies can establish robust and flexible technology backbones that drive lasting growth and competitiveness in foreign markets. In the forthcoming chapters, we will examine further technology and innovation issues—emerging technologies, intellectual property (IP) protection and innovation governance—to help emerging-market companies achieve the best global technology and innovation practices amid unstoppable turbulence in the business environment.

# Chapter 9 Legal and Ethical Risks

Emerging market companies that want to expand into foreign markets often face many legal and ethical challenges that must be managed carefully, or they risk damaging their reputations and their ability to operate successfully over the long term. Compliance with local laws and regulations is just the starting point. To succeed and prosper globally, entrepreneurs must also build ethical businesses and embrace corporate social responsibility. The legal and ethical dimensions of global expansion are complex and constantly evolving, creating a daunting and often intimidating environment for entrepreneurs. In this chapter, we will examine some of the most frequent legal and ethical mistakes made by emerging market companies and we will suggest strategies for avoiding these pitfalls.

One of the most crucial legal complications faced by firms expanding into emerging markets is the grasp and implementation of local legal systems and legal requirements in foreign markets. Many firms underestimate the intricacy and significance of local legal systems that are in place leading to non-compliance and problem legal liabilities.

An issue is a lack of sufficient legal due diligence. Numerous emerging market firms undertake insufficient legal due diligence when they enter foreign markets, failing to investigate laws and regulations in the local markets they wish to enter, obtaining required licenses and permits, and crafting the right legal contracts and agreements. Not doing proper legal due diligence can lead to expensive legal problems and fines and harm a company's reputation.

Yet another mistake to avoid is disregarding intellectual property (IP) safeguards. In numerous developing markets, IP regulations and remedies function differently than in developed markets: patent and trademark protection may be less secure or even inadequate, and the remedies available for IP infringement could be more limited. If companies do not take time to understand and secure their IP assets, they can see a loss of market share, revenue, and competitive advantage.

The companies that wish to avoid these traps must place importance on legal risk management and legal compliance as a part of their global expansion strategy. It is advised that these companies conduct remarkable legal due diligence; and employ local legal experts and advisors and insist on local language lawyers reviewing, drafting and concluding contracts. Set up the active compliance program and make sure that this program meets local requirements and international standards. Invest in IP protection strategies, such as registering your trademarks and patents in the local jurisdictions and develop a plan to enforce IP by taking legal action. You should also be aware of international IP treaties and agreements.

Failing to Adhere to Ethical Business Practices Yet another legal and ethical mistake commonly made by emerging market companies is failing to adhere to ethical business practices and standards in foreign markets. Many companies face pressure to engage in unethical or corrupt practices in order to gain a competitive advantage or deal with the complexities of local business environments. This can lead to legal and reputational risks.

Local business ethics, as well as corporate governance standards, are among the acute risks involved with any foreign investment. Different cultures and markets have different norms and standards of business practice. While local standards can vary significantly from what is considered appropriate in one's home country, their violation can range from innocent misunderstanding to criminal behavior. For example, gift-giving or hospitality norms vary from nation to nation; the obvious or hidden reason and nature of the gift might differ greatly. Problems can arise if a gift is given or received with innocent intention, but the practices of the target company ban such behavior. These actions themselves are an ethics issue. Brazilian state-run oil giant Petrobras was rocked by scandal in 2014 and 2015 when it emerged that Sergio Machado, CEO of transportation company Transpetro, part of the Petrobras group, had embezzled funds to bribe politicians and parties and to pay for prostitutes via UNAUTHORIZED offshore accounts in Panama. Clearly, Transpetro has a unique culture of spending on strippers at work, and that at best represented a serious conflict of interest for Machado.

More urgently for investors, such behavior raises the specter of misreporting one's debt on the one hand, and bribery that could undermine contracts and permits, on the other; certainly, Petrobras has enough of each of those problems without another. It was, in the end, alcohol and hookers that led to Machado's downfall. But that should hardly have been the first warning sign for ETHICS-MINDED investors.

Another trap is leaving unconsidered the field of corporate social responsibility (CSR) and sustainability. When penetrating emerging markets one faces an entire variety of social and environmental perils like living beneath the poverty line, inequality, and climate change. When a firm fails to consummate corporate social responsibility and sustainability while internationalizing they find themselves in the opposite role where instead of attracting the benediction of the public they garner ill fame by evoking social and environmental denigration by individuals ultimately facing worse resentment not only in public but eventually from the stakeholders and incitement of imprecations.

To prevent falling into these traps, emerging market companies must construct and effectuate rigorous ethical business practices and standards that conform to local behavioral norms and anticipations. This could involve constructing and enforcing a global code of conduct, presenting ethics and compliance training to employees, and arranging internal controls and reporting mechanisms to spot and stop misbehavior. It could also insist on fusing CSR and sustainability factors into business strategies and activities, such as executing social and environmental impact assessments, connecting to local communities and stakeholders, and publishing CSR and sustainability processes and outcomes.

Another challenge faced frequently by companies in emerging markets is risk management and crisis response. They often underrate both the chance of legal and ethical risks and crises in the first place and the magnitude of their consequences on the other. To the companies that lack relevant understanding, they tend to invest too little in the construction and maintenance of their legal, ethical and crisis response departments. They don't have enough information about the laws and regulations in different countries as well as the cultural differences, which makes it hard to deal with the unexpected problems in those regions.

One mistake is not being able to account and mitigate overall risks. Many emerging market companies do not develop thorough risk assessments that identify and rank legal and ethical risks in foreign markets, such as corruption, human rights abuses, or environmental disasters. Companies that operate without risk mitigation plans could experience preventable legal issues and public relations crises of major proportions.

Another mistake could be inadequate crisis management and a lack of foreign market crisis response. Many to-be emerging market companies are not equipped with the structure, the funding, or the expertise to manage timely, lawful and ethical crises. They can be product recall, cyber-crime or PR social media crises. These issues will stay long and the cost will get higher even if the company doesn't have legitimate crisis management. The response would stay long and costly. It could be even more expensive than experiencing a crisis if the company hasn't real crisis management.

To mitigate these risks, emerging market companies should make risk management and crisis response a crucial element of their global legal and ethical approach. This may require conducting regular risk appraisals and scenario planning routines, constructing and examining crisis management and response plans, and forming distinct crisis management teams and budgets. It may also mandate adopting risk management and crisis response skills including risk management software, emergency communication instruments, and worker education and rehearsals.

By tackling these legal and ethical dilemmas upfront, facing them head-on and implementing the appropriate strategies, resources, and precautions, emerging-market companies can navigate the complex legal and ethical landscape of globalization with skill and integrity. More legal and ethical considerations will be discussed in the chapters that follow, including anti-bribery and anti-corruption laws and practices, challenges to labor and human rights, and environmental sustainability, thereby offering a thorough exploration of the legal and ethical landscape within which emerging-market companies must operate on the global stage.

# CHAPTER 10: DEFICIENT RISK ASSESSMENT AND MITIGATION

Strategically evaluating and adequately managing risks is one of the fundamental elements determining whether or not a firm will successfully grow globally. As corporations expand into newer markets, the danger of jeopardizing their intended corporate strategy, financial performance and image drastically escalates. Firms that lack a process for determining, assessing, and containing these risks suffer from catastrophes. This portion of the article will illustrate the common mistakes made by corporations in emerging markets in their risk management efforts as well as how to suppress these risks.

One of the largest mistakes made by these firms is the lack of a thorough risk assessment of the political and economic and social aspects of, not only the new market but also the government entity with which they will be working. Many firms simply rush into the expansion resulting in a lack of foresight and hurriedly executed strategies.

Political risks can have a major influence on the business functionality within the foreign market. Some examples of political risks include changes in government policies, market conditions, and international relationships. Economic risks are closely related to the state economy. It can lead to a company's economic power and vigorousness affected by exchange rate volatility, inflation, and similar economic instability. Social risks arise due to the diversity of cultures and people. These risks can consist of cultural and ethical differences, disputes regarding labor practices, and attitudes toward foreign companies' products and productions. These risks in the business functionality can trigger other exposures.

To mitigate these risks, emerging-market firms should conduct well-designed risk assessments that deeply evaluate the political, economic, and social climates of the target market. This should involve gathering and analyzing data from diverse sources, such as governmental reports, industry publications, local media, and field intelligence. Furthermore, firms should consult indigenous experts, including political risk experts, economic analysts, and cultural inquirers, to gain better discernment of the market's unique challenges and opportunities.

Misunderstanding the Effects of Currency Fluctuations and International Currency Risks Like multinational corporations that operate globally, many organizations that conduct business in emerging economies regularly underestimate the effects of currency fluctuations and the risks associated with international currencies. This oversight typically involves failure to protect against currency risks as well as to implement tactical alternatives that can help minimize associated losses/reductions in income from variations in the exchange rates.

The financial effects of currency fluctuations can be significant on a company's revenue, costs, and profitability, especially when it engages in cross-border transactions and has investments overseas. For example, if a company earns revenue in a foreign currency that decreases in value relative to its home currency, the company will experience a fx 'translation effect to reported earnings and cash flows when the foreign currency is converted back to the domestic one-(measures of growth less one-time effects, For example, if the US dollar depreciates relative to the British pound, US-based companies with majority sales and profits in the US will convert those lower proceeds. Similarly, if a company bears expenses in foreign currencies and the domestic currency appreciates against those currencies, it will face higher expenses and narrower margins.

In order to reduce these risks, emerging market firms must create sound foreign exchange risk management strategies that are in line with their global expansion goals and risk tolerance. This could include using derivative hedging tools like options, forward contracts, and swaps to fix beneficial exchange rates and trim down reliance on exchange rate swings. It might also mean functioning in multiple currencies and markets and keeping a reasonable stash of foreign currencies to weather any short-term instability.

One of the most common mistakes that cause multinational organizations to fail in developing markets is ignoring the need to provide resilience to them. All too often, companies don't consider potential disruptions or "crises" - economic, supply, environmental, political, or sudden shocks such as category-5 hurricanes.

However, expanding globally opens companies up to a wide array of unpredictable risks that can disturb their supply chains, production cycles, and distribution connections. A devastating disaster like an earthquake, hurricane, flood, or tsunami, can plague a company by putting critical infrastructure or assets out of commission as well as making it challenging to transport goods from place to place. Moreover, political incidents such as trade conflicts, civil war and sanctions have the ability to disrupt a supply chain and impose a huge operational and financial risk to the corporate sector.

In order to mitigate these risks, emerging-market companies should prepare detailed contingency plans that identify various disruptive scenarios, assess their probability and impact, and outline clear responses and recovery strategies. At a minimum, these plans comprise a set of guidelines for alternate sourcing, production, and distribution coupled with a tailored governance, partnership, and decision-making framework during the crisis. They should also enhance the robustness and agility of the supply chain to improve resilience, such as through a wider base of suppliers, the maintenance of ample buffers, and a real-time dashboard using computerized or digital sensors to enhance responsiveness and visibility.

Ignoring the Need for Intellectual Property Protection and Cybersecurity Precautions

Finally, the relevance of IP protection and cybersecurity measures is overlooked by many firms from newly developed markets on their path to internationalization. In today's knowledge-driven economy, the patents, trademarks, and trade secrets of a company often make up its most valuable and differentiating assets. Astonishingly, however, many companies do not sufficiently secure their IP when venturing into different countries, leaving them susceptible to piracy, theft, and damage to their brand reputation.

Similarly, as companies digitize operations and increasingly employ technology and data to drive their global expansion efforts, they are also becoming increasingly exposed to cybersecurity risks, such as data breaches, cyber-attacks, and systems failures. Numerous firms still do not fully appreciate how sophisticated and pervasive cyber-attacks are in overseas markets, particularly in emerging markets where weak cybersecurity regulations and infrastructure create a target-rich environment.

In order to reduce such risks, companies operating in emerging markets should consider intellectual property (IP) protection and cybersecurity as an integral part of their overall global risk management scheme. This entails conducting IP audits and filings in selected locations, setting up strict IP policies and procedures, as well as monitoring and enforcing IP rights through court and administrative actions. Additionally, organizations should invest in reliable cybersecurity measures, such as data encryption, access control mechanisms, incident response plans, and employee education and training initiatives.

All in all, failing to properly assess risk and adequately mitigate risk upfront is a strong reason why these companies will be severely hamstrung due to their global expansion ambitions in emerging markets. Through prescient risk assessments, a steadfast contingency plan, and intrepid intellectual property (IP) protection and cyber security, they will be able to navigate the labyrinthine, fluid world of international business ably, and in so doing, rightly demand the rich proceeds of lasting prosperity and growth. Stay with us as we decry faddish short-termism and diffusion in the quest for global expansion.

# Chapter 11: Short-term Thinking

Emerging market companies experience a number of considerable challenges as they go about global expansion, one of the most important of which is the tendency for short-term considerations to eclipse long-term strategic goals. In the race to extract as much as possible from new market opportunities and to achieve rapid expansion, many companies unknowingly fall into the trap of making decisions based on immediate returns rather than the long-run purpose of their business. This short-term orientation and lack of strategic vision can undermine the sustainability and success of a company's global expansion efforts. In this chapter, we will examine the typical errors associated with short-term thinking and offer some approaches to the development of a clear and flexible vision of where in the world it should go.

Too many emerging market companies focus too much on short-term financial gains and ignore the long-term sustainability of their global operations. They put quick market entry and sales growth in front of "building the organization's foundation for long-term success." That means investments in talent development, partnerships, and customer loyalty are needed for long-term profitability.

Taking this perspective has multiple detrimental outcomes. Firms can make decisions that are somewhat asinine due to obscure or incomplete data, like penetrating markets with probable short-term prospects or partnering with ventures that have diverse objectives. They may also disregard the growth of long-lasting infrastructure and capabilities that permit a firm to develop in new markets, such as constructing a local management crew or setting up a reliable supply chain and selling channels. Finally, they can also destroy the innovation systems and the relationships between critical new market stakeholders, such as consumers, realtors, or homeland communities by primarily pursuing the short-term gain instead of creating the long-run value or the company clearly doesn't know how to manage the overseas business.

So as to avoid these problems, companies from emerging markets are required to make decisions that have to do with sustainability as their first priority and adopt an attitude on a long-term basis where global expansion strategies are concerned. What could be counted in this regard is the establishment of long-term objectives which could be measured and which could be further maintained by objectives such as market share, customer contentment as well as the realization of social impact goals. This could be aligned through short-term courses of action which in turn could be invested in. From another point of view, firms should also have the ability to build up strong local teams, which apart from anything else can be built through training and development programs. It is in this regard that successive benefits can be achieved through succession planning processes, which are also accounted for within the decision firms. What also counts here is to be able to receive feedback from stakeholders, based on this. feedback firms would be able to build into, the conclusions that they make as far as long-term decisions are concerned, and therefore it is through this realization that strong building blocks could be built that- when added together would form a better vision of what companies in general are supposed to achieve.

Another typical mistake that companies from developing nations make is that they lack a strong international strategy that is flexible enough to adapt to their core competencies and values. Many companies drive on international opportunities in the course of their expansion while at the same time entering multiple international markets as well as permitting several international initiatives without being able to benefit from a clear strategic framework and direction. The lack of strategic clarity often results in the unproductive and incoherent distribution of various resources and, in turn, a lack of a sharp focus and differentiation in the marketplace.

In addition, with the rapid transformations and uncertainties in world business today, firms must be able to respond to new challenges and openings by realigning their strategies. Nevertheless, many companies in emerging markets find it difficult to create the necessary strategic agility and adaptability. Often their predicaments flow from inflexible organizational structures, decision-making processes, and cultural values.

Stability, not innovation and constant readjustment, is what their structures, the way they have always made decisions, and their cultures prioritize.

In order to solve these issues, emerging market firms need to establish a sharp and captivating global strategy that lays out the specifics of their unmatched value proposition, target markets and competitive advantages. This strategy should be backed by a meticulous analysis of the company's strengths, weaknesses, opportunities and threats on the global stage as well as a detailed awareness of the customers' needs, the market trends and the competitive situation. Companies should likewise establish some strategic agility within their firms that includes fostering a culture of experiments and learning, giving autonomy to the local teams to make decisions and adapt to the changes and utilizing digital technologies and analytics to enhance their strategic decision-making as well as responsiveness.

The one-third mistake that I have often seen new market companies make is underestimating the importance of building strong brand equity and customer loyalty in new markets. Many companies assume that their products or services will automatically be attractive to local customers based on their price or functionality, without investing in building a strong and differentiated brand identity that resonates with local culture and values.

However, to generate long-term value and differentiate in the modern era's globalized and hyper-competitive business environment, achieving market strength is indispensable. Market strengths can, accordingly, raise prices; create customer loyalty; and protect from competition and disruption. Particularly, business strength and customer loyalty are the best strategies for a successful emergence market in which trust and relationship are the most effective tools.

In order to create durable brand equity and customer loyalty in new markets, companies in emerging markets need to spend time and money going deep into what their customers value most and developing brand positioning and messaging that really resonates with local consumers. These efforts may involve commissioning market research, cultivating relationships with local opinion-makers or celebrities, and differentiating their messaging and brand look and feel through culturally relevant nods made within packaging, advertisements, and logos. Additionally, companies must focus relentlessly on driving customer satisfaction, whether by guaranteeing excellent customer service, operating with agility to capture and act on customer feedback or concerns, or mapping personalized and engaging customer journeys across touchpoints and channels.

Finally, many companies in emerging markets don't invest in research and development (R&D) to drive innovation. They focus on shrinking their cost gaps and extending their business models to other emerging markets—both useful but potentially devastating moves in some sectors. But many companies also retreat to these moves because the more aggressive their moves, the easier they are to imitate. They focus too much on unit cost reductions at the expense of investing in the skills and capabilities required to deliver better performance.

Nevertheless, in the rapid and disturbed business environment of today, innovation is a capital force for growth in the long term and competitiveness. Companies not innovating stand at risk of sliding behind more nimble and imaginative rivals, to missing out on fresh market prospects and customer needs. Moreover, innovation can be vital to build differentiation and loyalty and ameliorate social and environmental troubles in many emerging markets with more and more demanding and sophisticated customers.

To spur innovation and stay ahead of rivals, companies in emerging markets need to give priority to R&D, and embed innovation deep in their global strategies and operations. This means setting aggressive innovation goals and metrics, allocating dedicated resources and budgets for R&D, and building a culture of creativity, experimentation, and calculated risk-taking across the organization. Companies should actively engage with local innovation ecosystems, such as universities, research institutes, and startups, to tap into fresh ideas, talent, and technologies, and to co-create solutions that meet local needs and opportunities.

To sum up, the lack of strategy and the minimization of the time limit can injure the joining of the global market in the long term for emerging market companies. By developing a sustainable global strategy, measuring the regulations around the globe, evaluating and responding to risk, building brand equity and genuine customers, and invest customer relationship management system, CRM or global innovation management, companies can increase sustainability, avoid bankruptcy in joining the global market, and get the fame from the global market.

# Chapter 12: Summary and Prospects

We have looked at several challenges and opportunities emerging market companies encounter as they globalize. From reconciling clashing cultures and tailoring go-to-market strategies to creating partnerships and running complex supply chains, the path to global triumph offers myriad potential pitfalls and stumbles. But by absorbing others' stories and pursuing a disciplined, strategic approach to globalization, emerging market companies can set themselves on course for long-term growth and success in today's global business landscape.

Summary of Common Mistakes and Important Lessons

1. In prior sections, we've discussed and dissected several of the primary blunders that emerging market firms tend to make while going worldwide. These consist of:
2. Neglecting to engage in an in-depth market research process and proper due diligence
3. Failing to appreciate the significance of cultural adjustment and localization
4. Fail to create solid alliances and coalitions at a local level
5. Overestimating how easily one business model or management practice can be transported to other places may be one of the single biggest reasons why so many companies have trouble implementing strategies, transferring technologies, or learning from their experiences.
6. Mismanagement of financial resources and exposure to financial risks.
7. Not investing in developing and retaining talent
8. Failing to put social and environmental sustainability measures on top of the agenda
9. Not realizing the importance of creating brand recognition and retaining customers
10. Not innovating and adapting to changing market conditions

11. No clear and convincing growth vision and corresponding strategy

To improve their prospects for success in the global arena, emerging-market companies should understand and avoid these common pitfalls and incorporate the key learnings and best practices highlighted throughout this book. Some of the most important learnings include:

1. Conduct comprehensive market research and scientific due diligence to support strategic decision-making.
2. Modify products, services, and even business models to meet the preferences of the local market.
3. Recruit robust local teams and alliances to manage social and statutory intricacies
4. Create an unambiguous and persuasive worldwide brand and value offer.
5. Invest in innovation, research and development
6. Set the company's social and environmental sustainability as a priority.
7. Adopt flexibility and adjustability in response to fluctuations in market situations and potential advantages.
8. Strike a balance between the immediate and the long-term.

The Changing Face of Global Business Expansion Going forward, it is quite apparent that global business will continue to change and new challenges and opportunities will be presented for companies from emerging markets to expand their global presence. A few of the key trends and factors that will shape the future of global expansion are:

1. The basic operational and global competitive model is being altered fundamentally by digitization.
2. Global brands must integrate within their organizational structures worldwide sustainability and social responsibility to account for consumer and investor demands.

3. The global economic and political landscape is being fundamentally altered as emerging markets rapidly rise.
4. Globally fragmented supply chains are rapidly experiencing ever-growing risks and disruptions at higher and higher velocities.
5. The worldwide talent and resource race accelerates as companies search globally for the diverse and high-performing team members required to innovate and grow.

In order to succeed in such a quickly changing and complex global environment, aspiring leading companies from emerging markets now need to be more agile, flexible and creative than ever. They need to use digital technologies and data analytics to understand customer needs and market dynamics, and then optimize operations and supply chains. They need to build strong and reputable brands that resonate globally and mirror the values and aspirations of their customers. They need to have a culture of continuous learning, trying and teaming, in order to be pre-emptive and capture new opportunities.

There are a number of exciting opportunities and trends on the horizon that emerging market companies can exploit to fuel global growth and competitiveness. Some examples are enumerated below.

1. Companies can differentiate themselves and attract loyal, socially conscious customers by offering sustainable products and services in response to rising consumer demand for green and ethical choices.
2. Thanks to the proliferation of digital platforms and technologies in developing economies, companies can skip cumbersome stages of development and link into global markets faster than ever before, reaching new customers and creating fresh opportunities to raise productivity and growth.
3. The increase in the number of middle-class consumers around the world—especially in Asia and Africa—who desire higher-quality, more affordable goods and services.
4. The rise of South-South trade and investment, a crucial outcome of a world no longer dominated by advanced economies that

account for a smaller share of global activity and contribution to global growth than at any time during the past five decades.
5. The development of new business models and ecosystems, such as sharing and circular economies, that represent a basic change in the way goods and services are produced and used, resulting in unforeseen opportunities for value creation and capture.

Strategic Advices

Not only can emerging market companies succeed in the global marketplace, they can change it for the better. By adhering to these principles and strategies. By staying true to their core values and purposes. They can open up new possibilities for growth and development, not only for themselves but also for the communities and societies they serve. They can fuel innovation and progress, not only within their own sectors but throughout the world. And they can help to build a more sustainable, inclusive, and prosperous future, not only for their own stakeholders but for all of humanity.

So let's meet the challenges and embrace the opportunities of global expansion with courage, curiosity, and determination. Let's learn from the past, but also look to the future with confidence and resolve. And let's, together, beyond borders and divides, imagine a better world for everyone.

# ACKNOWLEDGEMENT

In the creation of this seminal series, I have had the distinct privilege of drawing upon the invaluable experiences, insights, and expertise generously shared by a distinguished global network of esteemed partners and accomplished friends. Their direct and indirect contributions have been instrumental, and it is with profound gratitude that I acknowledge the indelible influence they have had on this work.

Kanth Krishnan: Managing Director at Accenture, has been a beacon of inspiration with his incisive insights and visionary leadership in technology services. His profound depth of knowledge and innovative approach have significantly enriched the content of this book.

As Managing Director at Newmark, Jeff Pappas has provided critical perspectives on the dynamic global real estate market landscape. His unparalleled expertise has contributed to a deeper understanding of the business environments explored herein.

Haitao Qi, Chairman of Devott Research and Advisory, has provided exceptionally enlightening perspectives on technology innovations and market trends, especially in the Asian context.

Formerly leading Outsourcing and Managed Services at PwC, Charles Aird's comprehensive knowledge and strategic foresight in outsourcing services have greatly contributed to my understanding of this critical business function.

Mike Beares: Founder and Board Chairman of Clutch.co, has been instrumental in shaping my views on business connectivity through his entrepreneurial spirit and dedication to bridging businesses with the optimal service providers.

It has been my great privilege to learn from and collaborate with these distinguished individuals and institutions operating at the leading edge of our industry. Any merits of this book stem directly from the exceptional global network of friends and partners upon whom I rely. Any faults or shortcomings are solely my own.

Last, but not the least, the unwavering understanding and support of my beloved wife, Biyu, has been an inspiration to this professional endeavor. The intensive writing workload harkened back to my doctoral dissertation at Yale a quarter-century ago. She remains the driving force behind my career growth and personal fulfillment.

# ABOUT THE AUTHOR

## Stephan S. Sunn

Stephan Sunn is the Executive Partner at Sanford Black Advisory, a preeminent global business and investment consultancy. In this capacity, he collaborates with industry leaders to advise companies worldwide on growth strategy, marketing/sales, innovation monetization, partnerships, and mergers & acquisitions. Over the past two decades, Mr. Sunn has consulted on sourcing provider selection for more than 30 international corporations and over 20 investment and M&A deals in the technology services, digital technologies, and global outsourcing sectors.

Mr. Sunn possesses particular expertise in empowering private enterprises to accelerate growth and enhance value creation through engagement with governments and technology parks. He holds a leadership position with Devott Co., China's largest private research firm focused on the IT, software, and technology services industries. Additionally, he serves as a Director at the China IT and Outsourcing Association. His clients span Fortune 500 companies, state-owned enterprises, technology parks, SMBs, and startups in both developed and emerging markets.

A graduate of the University of Science and Technology of China (USTC) with a Bachelor of Science degree, and Yale University with a Master of Science and Ph.D., Mr. Sunn frequently shares his insights and research as a speaker at global conferences and events. He is a prolific author and an accomplished presenter for his projects and clients around the world.

# BOOKS BY THIS AUTHOR

## Competing For The Growth

This book serves as a guidebook for city planners, economic development professionals, tech park builders, and public officials who aim to create thriving innovation communities that attract global trade and stimulate investments. It offers a structured path that begins with intangible factors like vision setting and partnership alignment and extends to pilots and full-blown magnet programs.

The book provides real-life instructions to help put these ideas into practice, including effective strategies for attracting rapidly growing businesses and talent, creating a setting that promotes innovation and entrepreneurship, fostering a competitive and appealing business climate, and building a globally recognized brand and reputation.

The author emphasizes that cities and tech parks must play to their strengths and assets to compete and win in the global arena. The race for relevance is on, and the window of opportunity to determine the outcome is closing. Cities and companies have what they need to succeed, and with the options, relationships, and guidance provided in this book, city managers and tech park authorities can make the decisions necessary to lead their communities to success in the world investment and trade arena.

## Searching The New Profits

In the face of global market turbulence and domestic uncertainties, American small and medium-sized businesses (SMBs) and startups have significant growth opportunities in emerging markets. However, these markets also present unique challenges. This handbook provides a semi-analytical and semi-prescriptive approach to help American SMBs and entrepreneurs succeed in these rapidly expanding markets. Conversely, governments, technology parks, and corporations in emerging countries can utilize this book to learn how to collaborate with U.S. companies in their markets to serve their customers effectively.

The book covers essential themes such as researching and identifying matching markets, choosing the appropriate market entry mode, local marketing and sales tactics, effective risk management, establishing an active and reputable presence in the local market, ensuring full legal compliance, avoiding political involvement, talent search and retention, and balancing standardization and localization. The final chapter shares valuable lessons from decades of business practices, acknowledging that readers may have different perspectives on these topics. Expanding knowledge through diverse viewpoints is beneficial for U.S. SMB and startup leaders. Despite the challenges, penetrating foreign markets can be highly profitable, and U.S. enterprises have a reasonable chance of success by capitalizing on the vast potential of these rapidly growing territories.

## Cracking The Winning Codes

This book serves as a comprehensive guide for international technology and outsourcing companies seeking to enter and succeed in the highly competitive U.S. market. It emphasizes the importance of adapting to the unique American business culture, which values innovation, diversity, relationships, customer-centricity, and results-oriented management. The guide highlights the need to navigate the complex U.S. regulatory landscape, including federal and state laws, as well as key legislations such as FCPA, SOX, and HIPAA.

The book covers essential topics such as understanding American business culture, complying with legal requirements, developing effective marketing strategies, employing successful sales techniques, addressing cultural differences, and managing risks associated with entering a new market.

Additionally, it encourages the use of innovative tactics to differentiate from competitors and gain market share.

A special section titled "The Lessons" shares the author's personal experiences and insights, providing practical execution tips that focus on solution-oriented approaches, leveraging referrals and testimonials, managing communication costs, delivering higher quality than promised, and investing in proven local sales leaders.

By adhering to the core principles of understanding buyer preferences, continuous innovation, human capital development, risk management, customer-centricity, and resilient operations, global providers can successfully navigate and thrive in the lucrative U.S. market.

## Win More Businesses

In the digital age, businesses must navigate the complex landscape of Marketing Technology (Martech) and Sales Technology (Salestech) to stay competitive and drive growth. "Win More Deals in Global Markets" provides a comprehensive guide for leveraging these technologies to enhance customer experiences, streamline processes, and boost revenue across international markets. The book explores the convergence of marketing, sales, and technology, emphasizing the importance of data-driven decision-making and cross-functional collaboration. It offers strategies for overcoming challenges in digital transformation, such as resistance to change and skills gaps, while also addressing the unique considerations of global expansion and localization. The authors predict future trends in Martech and Salestech, including the increasing role of AI, personalization, and emerging technologies like AR/VR and voice interfaces. Through real-world success stories from global brands like Coca-Cola, Sephora, and Airbnb, readers gain valuable insights into harnessing the power of these technologies for business success. This book serves as an essential resource for executives and professionals seeking to navigate the digital ecosystem and drive growth in the international marketplace.

# Renovations Or Revolutions

The book "Renovation or Revolution? Impacts of Latest AI on BPO and Contact-centers Industries" provides an in-depth exploration of the transformative potential of artificial intelligence (AI) within the business process outsourcing (BPO) and contact center industries. It emphasizes the importance of early adoption, customization, and localization of AI solutions to gain a competitive edge in the global marketplace. The book highlights the evolving role of human agents, who will focus on complex problem-solving and relationship-building, while AI handles routine tasks. It also discusses the development of AI expertise within organizations and the ethical considerations surrounding AI implementation. The authors present a roadmap for incorporating AI, underlining the need for a clear vision, employee training, and continuous improvement. Looking ahead, the book envisions a future of collaborative human-AI partnerships, hyper-personalization, and proactive customer engagement. It stresses that embracing AI is crucial for BPO and contact center companies to achieve sustainable growth and remain competitive in the international arena. The book serves as a comprehensive guide for executives navigating the AI revolution in the global business services industry.

www.ingramcontent.com/pod-product-compliance
Lightning Source LLC
Chambersburg PA
CBHW072000210526
45479CB00003B/1014